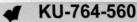

## ADVERTISING VEHICLE

Many vans and trucks have advertising on their sides, but look out for unusual adverts. It could be a car with a gigantic drinks can on the back or, maybe, something like this Renault van in a cow disguise, complete with horns on the roof, door mirrors shaped like ears and eyebrows over the headlights!

 **I - SPY points: 35**

## AMBULANCE

Ambulances are covered in a bright, eye-catching and reflective livery that, along with flashing lights, warns other drivers to let them pass by on the way to an emergency, or rushing to a hospital. All police/ambulance/fire vehicles display blue flashing lights.

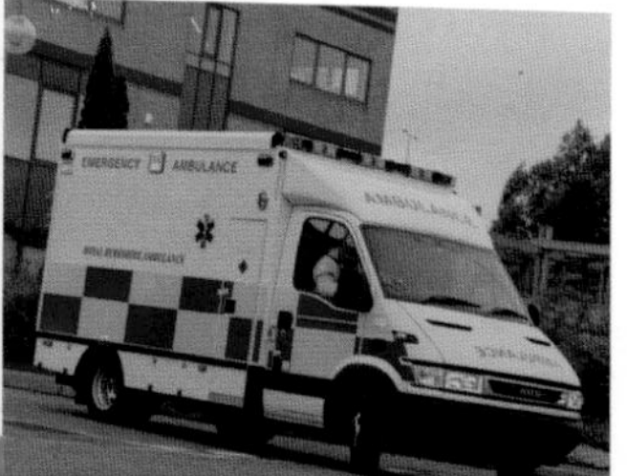

 **I - SPY points: 15**

## ARTICULATED TRUCK

One of the largest vehicles found regularly on the road. A front tractor cab unit pulls a trailer with two, four or six wheels; this trailer can be flat with a visible load, or with its cargo enclosed.

I - SPY points: 10

## BENDY BUS

These articulated buses can be seen in London and many airports. They pivot in the middle and are known as bendy buses. More passengers can be accommodated inside them than standard single-decker buses.

I - SPY points: 20

# BICYCLE

The typical bike has a triangulated frame which gives it the strength to support the rider, and wheels with lots of spokes that spread the impact from the road through the tyres. A mountain bike like this one has knobbly tyres so it can be ridden over rough ground.

I - SPY points: 10

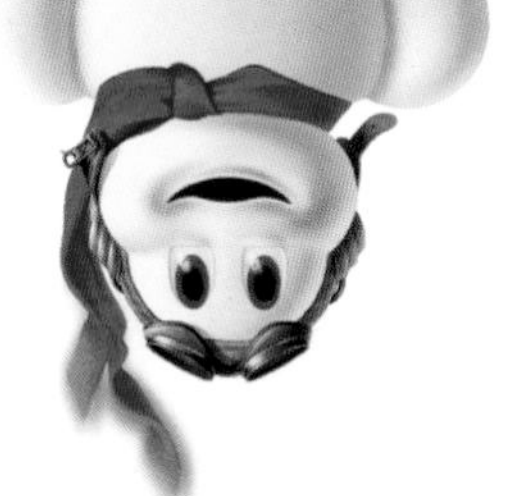

# BLOOD/ORGAN DELIVERY BIKE

Because it's manoeuvrable and unlikely to be held up in traffic jams, a powerful motorbike is the best way to get urgent materials to a hospital. This could be blood or even a body organ, such as a heart, that might save someone's life.

I - SPY points: 40

## BOAT TRAILER

 I - SPY points: 20

Many kinds of trailers are available to transport boats. They vary with the size and weight of the craft, from simple frames for a small dinghy to large, multi-wheel models that can transport a powerboat or even a small yacht.

## BUS, DOUBLE-DECKER

Buses with an upstairs compartment operate in every part of Britain. They're big, rectangular and able to carry lots of people. Almost all have two sets of doors, the front ones for entrance and the rear ones for exit to help passengers flow on and off.

 I - SPY points: 10

## BUS, SINGLE-DECKER

You'll see single-deck buses everywhere, smaller ones sometimes have one set of doors for passengers, while larger ones have two. This petrol-electric hybrid example is operated by Transport For London, whose buses are all painted red.

 **I - SPY points: 10**

## CAMPER VAN

This compact mobile home is adapted from an ordinary minibus. You'll be able to tell a camper from a minibus by looking at the roof: camper vans generally have an extendable roof that extends upwards so you can stand up inside them, when parked. Even when folded flat, you can still see it.

 **I - SPY points: 15**

## CAR REMOVAL TRUCK

This lorry has a platform at the back called a flatbed, and its own crane with a 'grabber'. This is used to hoist a car into the air, using slings around its tyres, and swing it round on to the flatbed. You might see one removing a crashed car ... or an illegally-parked car in a city centre!

 I - SPY points: 25

## CAR TRAILER

One way to transport two cars with just one driver is to use a car trailer. These trailers are made from strong welded metal so they can support the weight of the car. An electric cable, also plugged into the tow-car, powers the trailer's rear lights.

# CAR TRANSPORTER

These incredible articulated trucks can carry several cars – usually brand new ones being delivered to garages – on up to three levels. The cars are driven on to the back of the transporter and then locked into place; they look like they might fall off but are safely secured!

 I - SPY points: 20

# CARAVAN

Owning a caravan means you can go on holiday and take your home with you, giving you freedom to stop anywhere you choose. The range of models is enormous, from tiny two-wheelers to four-wheeled mobile mansions! But they're all box-shaped, and almost always white or a similarly pale colour.

 I - SPY points: 15

# CARAVAN, FOLDING

A folding caravan has an upper section that retracts to reduce its height almost by half. The interior fittings cleverly interlock so nothing gets crushed. Owners like them because they can fit inside a garage and their low profile means a car uses less fuel when towing them.

 I - SPY points: 30

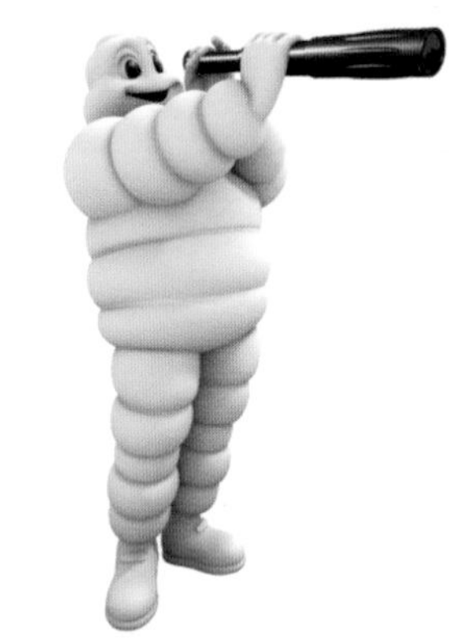

# CAR-DERIVED VAN

Not everyone who uses a van needs a large box-on-wheels. Many manufacturers offer a van based on a normal family car, such as this Vauxhall Corsavan. The body shell is the same as a normal car, but the rear side windows are replaced with metal panels, and instead of a rear seat there is a flat load area.

 I - SPY points: 10

## CATTLE TRAILER

You see these large trailers in the country, where farmers use them to move cattle as well as sheep or pigs. Slots in the sides allow plenty of air so the animals can breathe well, while twin axles give good stability on fields or rough tracks.

 **I - SPY points: 25**

## CONCRETE MIXER

If you see one of these large vehicles rumbling along the road, it's probably on its way to a building site. The huge drum at the back revolves as the truck drives along, keeping its mixture of sand, cement and water moving so it can be poured out at its destination as concrete.

 **I - SPY points: 20**

## CHERRYPICKER

This type of vehicle could be handy in orchards – its rising platform allows access to ripe fruit in treetops – hence the name. But they are used for all kinds of 'working at height' tasks, including repairs to streetlights and telegraph poles, and maintaining buildings. This one has extendable 'feet' that lift the vehicle off the ground, making it totally stable when the platform is raised.

I - SPY points: 25

## CITY CAR

These short, stubby cars are ideal for people who live in large towns and cities because they can make use of short gaps in traffic, tight parking spaces and usually have economic engines.

I - SPY points: 15

## CLASSIC CAR

Classic cars are those built from 1945 to around 1980 and have a loyal band of enthusiastic owners dedicated to keeping them going. Classics are often identifiable from their chrome trim and their often rounded styling.

 I - SPY points: 20

## COACH

There is never any standing room on a coach because it's not designed for constant stop/start operation. It takes passengers on specified journeys that can be quite long. There are comfortable seats, in pairs, along either side for a commanding view of the scenery.

 I - SPY points: 10

## CONTAINER TRUCK

These trucks, with flat rear trailers, are the last link in the global container shipping chain; cranes transfer the containers from cargo ships to the trucks, carrying all types of goods all over the world.

## CONVERTIBLE

This type of car has a roof in the form of a folding metal frame, covered with flexible canvas-type material. Some are electrically powered like this Mini, others need to be raised or lowered by hand, some convertibles now have folding metal roofs.

## COUPÉ

This Audi TT is a typical example of a coupé. It has a roofline that tapers to a finish at the very back of the car. Most coupés have a roof lower than a family car. But many still also have two small seats in the back.

**I - SPY points: 15**

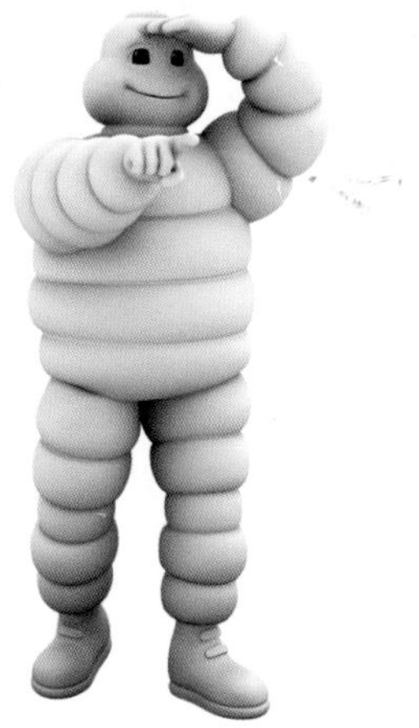

## CROSSOVER

A 'crossover' has a lower half that's like a 4x4 off-roader and an upper portion like a normal family hatchback or estate. Many come with four-wheel drive. This one is a Mazda CX-7 but other popular models include the Ford Kuga, Nissan Qashqai and Peugeot 3008.

**I - SPY points: 10**

## CURTAINSIDE TRUCK

This kind of truck is perfect for regular, small deliveries of heavy items. That's why they are popular with breweries transporting barrels of beer to a large number of pubs. The side curtains can be pulled aside easily so the heavy barrels can be unloaded from either side of the truck.

## DISABLED PERSON'S TRANSPORT

This multi-purpose vehicle has been modified to allow wheelchair access using a ramp. Sometimes the vehicles feature extended roofs so the wheelchair user is comfortable and has a good view.

## DOG HANDLER'S VAN

Dog handlers' vehicles look like any other van on the outside, apart from one key feature: a revolving roof-top ventilator, ensuring the animals travelling inside get enough fresh air and keep cool.

**I - SPY points: 25**

## )RAWBAR TRAILER

Veight and length restrictions ıean there are legal limits on the ize of articulated trucks on our oads. For bulky but light cargo, ıowever, a drawbar trailer – owed behind a truck with a igid chassis – can increase carrying capacity.

**I - SPY points: 20**

## DRIVING SCHOOL CAR

People learning to drive must display a square, white sticker on the front and back of the car with a large red capital 'L' on it; it stands for 'Learner'. Many driving school cars also have a large roof sign, like this one.

I - SPY points: 15

## DROPSIDE PICK-UP

Builders find these small trucks useful. At the rear is a flat load area on to which pallets of bricks, for example, can be loaded by a forklift truck. The side and rear panels then fold up and lock into place, to prevent anything sliding off when the truck is moving.

I - SPY points: 15

# ELECTRIC CITY CAR

This Reva G-Wiz is a tiny 100% electric-powered car, which classifies it as a 'zero-emission vehicle'. This means the owner is exempt from the London Congestion Charge, and can enjoy benefits like free parking and battery recharging.

**I - SPY points: 30**

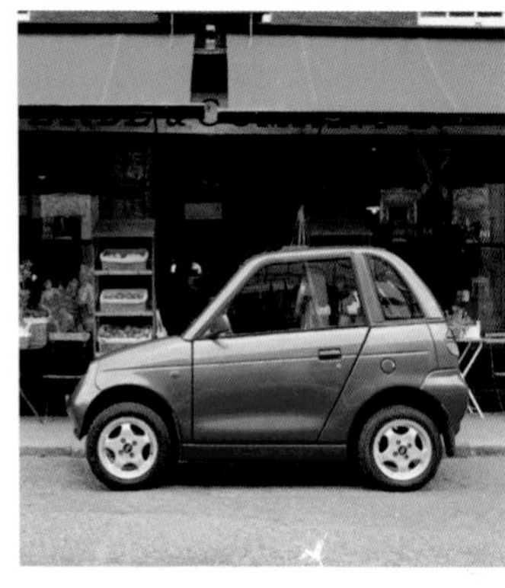

# EMERGENCY RESCUE VEHICLE

Although its cab is like the one you'll see on any delivery van, the rear part of this vehicle features a large, T-shaped bar that lowers electrically. After the front wheels of a broken-down car are placed on the bar, it can be lifted to safely tow it to a garage for repair.

**I - SPY points: 15**

## ESTATE CAR

This type of car is designed for dual-use. With the rear seats in the upright position, it's like any other family car, but with those rear seats folded flat, the square, boxy shape at the back helps it carry larger loads, like a van.

## EXCAVATOR

Its proper name is a 'back-hoe loader', which describes its two functions of being able to dig at one end and shovel at the other. But most people call it simply a JCB. It's the name of the company that makes most of them, and stands for JC Bamford, the man who invented it in 1953.

## EXECUTIVE CAR

People who have important positions in companies and other organisations often drive cars that look impressive, with large wheels and a prominent radiator grille. This Jaguar XF is a popular choice but other executive cars are made by BMW, Lexus, Mercedes-Benz amongst others.

**I - SPY points: 10**

## FASTRAC

JCB makes this powerful, four-wheel drive tractor that can also be used as a road vehicle, which is why it has full-width plastic mudguards fitted. It can be driven at 40mph on tarmac, much faster than conventional tractors, and can do all kinds of jobs, from ploughing to towing. You may see these on country roads travelling between farms.

**I - SPY points: 40**

## FIRE CONTROL UNIT

Britain's larger fire stations have a fleet of different vehicles for each incident. This VW Transporter is operated by the London Fire Brigade, as a fire investigation unit. It carries special equipment and staff trained to assess a situation before, during and after the fire itself.

I - SPY points: 30

## FIRE ENGINE, PUMP

Everyone calls them 'fire engines' but the main task of a vehicle like this is to act as a powerful pump. It carries its own water supply for putting out small fires and can also pump water from the mains supply. Lockers along the sides carry protective clothing and specialised rescue equipment, and carry ladders on top.

I - SPY points: 20

## FIRE ENGINE, TURNTABLE

This impressive vehicle is found in larger fire stations, especially in cities where there are many tall buildings. Although it carries fire-fighting equipment, its main job is to offer an escape route from upper storeys in buildings. The boom on the back can be raised upwards, so people can step to safety on to the platform on the end of it.

**I - SPY points: 30**

## FUEL TANKER

Bulk liquids are transported in specially-designed vehicles called tankers. They come in many sizes but some of the biggest, like this articulated, 12-wheeler DAF, are used to deliver fuels from refineries and depots to petrol stations. The tank itself is rounded, and shaped so that every last drop can be drained out of it. There are also tankers that are used to carry powder.

**I - SPY points: 10**

## GLASS VAN

It doesn't take much to shatter a sheet of glass, so transporting it can be difficult. Window companies use a van like this Citroën, with a specially-designed frame attached to its side that gently grips even very large glass panes so they arrive without breaking.

**I - SPY points: 20**

## GRITTER

On the back of this truck is a triangulated container, wide at the top and narrow at the bottom. It is filled with fine chunks of grit and, when moving, the driver spreads it on the road surface. A gritter is essential when roads are covered in snow or ice to keep vehicles moving.

**I - SPY points: 15**

## GT CAR

This car is a Maserati GranTurismo. It is built in Italy and is very fast. GranTurismo is the Italian for Grand Touring. GT sports cars can cover, or 'tour', long distances at high speed.

**I - SPY points: 20**

## HATCHBACK

A hatchback has an additional door across the rear end, opening on to a luggage space that can be doubled in volume if the rear seats are folded down. This Vauxhall Astra is one of the most popular in Britain, but most major manufacturers offer similar cars.

**I - SPY points: 5**

## HEARSE

A hearse is a specially lengthened type of large estate car used to carry a coffin. They often travel slowly and in convoy with other vehicles, containing relatives and friends. They're painted black but the coffin – which can be seen in the back – is usually covered in bright, cheerful flowers.

**I - SPY points: 25**

## HEAVY TRUCK

These lorries, called Large Goods Vehicles or HGVs, can have more than two axles; the one in the picture, used for transporting and unloading heavy building materials, has steering to the front two to help it get round tight corners.

**I - SPY points: 10**

## HIGHWAY/MOTORWAY MAINTENANCE TRUCK

This general-purpose truck helps to prepare major roads and motorways for disruptions and roadworks. It carries cones and barriers, and thanks to its powerful lighting rig at the back can act as a gigantic warning signal.

 **I - SPY points: 20**

## HORSEBOX

At first glance it might look like a removal van, but it has a ribbed ramp for a rear door that folds down so horses can be led easily inside. Many horseboxes also have a cosy compartment above the cab where riders can sleep at events a long way from home.

 **I - SPY points: 20**

## ICE-CREAM VAN

The brightly-painted vans have a tall rear end section where you can buy your ice-cream through a sliding window. Double points for one with a large model of an ice-cream cone on the roof.

 **I - SPY points: 10**

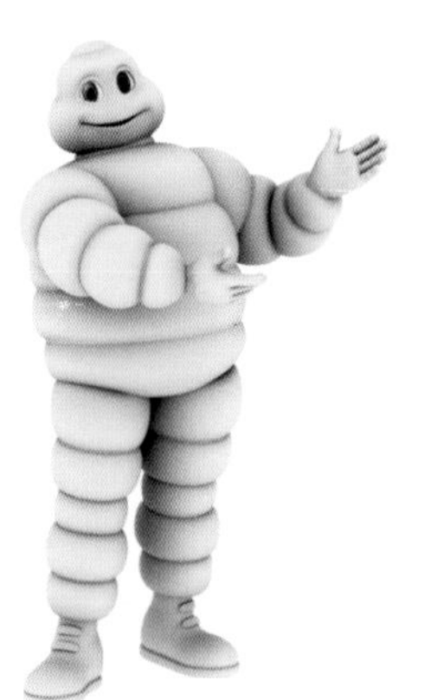

## KIT CAR

Very few people can afford an original classic sports-racing car from the 1950s or 1960s. But you can build a replica in your own garage. This is a Westfield Eleven kit car, a reproduction of a 1950s Lotus, and other popular kit cars build into copies of the Lotus Seven and AC Cobra.

 **I - SPY points: 25**

## LIGHT MILITARY VEHICLE, LAND ROVER

The original four-wheel drive, go-anywhere utility vehicle, a Land Rover is so versatile that it can be used on battle fields as well as farm fields. Double points for one in army camouflage paint.

**I - SPY points: 15**

## .IGHT MILITARY VEHICLE, ›INZGAUER

'hey are built with four or six vheels, all of which are driven ›o that the Pinzgauer, with its vast ȷround clearance, can negotiate ılmost any terrain. For this eason, they are popular with ɿe British Army, which owns ›everal hundred.

**I - SPY points: 35**

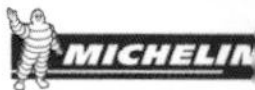

## LIGHT TRUCK

This Iveco Eurocargo, along with the DAF LF, is among the UK's most popular light trucks. They deliver all sorts of the things we need locally every day, such as fresh bread.

**I - SPY points: 10**

## LIMOUSINE

Many celebrities, like Simon Cowell, own one of these, a Maybach limousine. It's an extra-long saloon car with very wide doors and a luxurious interior. The owner is often driven by a chauffeur. Some limousines have an extra row of seats and an extra pair of doors.

**I - SPY points: 30**

## LONG-DISTANCE COACH

For long journeys perhaps from one country to another, special coaches are available. They tend to be very large vehicles with two decks of seats and on-board facilities including toilets and a kitchen to make the trip pleasant. Three axles make the ride more comfortable and allow a heavier payload. The lower rear section is used to carry luggage.

**I - SPY points: 10**

## LOW-LOADER

Very powerful 'tractor' units are needed to haul a low-loader trailer like this. It's a basic platform-on-wheels used for transporting heavy machinery or vehicles from place to place.

**I - SPY points: 20**

## LUTON VAN

A Luton van has a load area extending out above the passenger compartment. This type of van was created in Luton, Bedfordshire in the early 20th century. The town was Britain's hat-making centre, and the local manufacturers needed a van for carefully carrying headgear that was light but bulky.

**I - SPY points: 10**

## MICROCAR

These miniature cars come mostly from France. This one is called an Aixam, and Ligier is another brand sold in the UK. They're also known as 'quadricycles'. They have tiny engines that give very low fuel consumption, but they are slow, ideal in towns.

**I - SPY points: 30**

## MICROVAN

You will see many of these tiny delivery vans in use even though they're no longer sold new. The driver and passenger sit above the low-power engine, which puts the cab in the 'forward control' position. They're ideal for small businesses making daily deliveries in tight city streets.

**I - SPY points: 15**

## MILITARY TRUCK

The military operates these four-wheel drive trucks, which can haul either a load of equipment in the back or provide covered seating for 18 soldiers.

**I - SPY points: 30**

## MILK FLOAT

Here is a great opportunity for your I-Spy points total... but only if you're prepared to get up early and have good hearing! These near-silent electric vehicles deliver milk and other products in urban areas in the very early morning. During the daytime, they are recharged to be ready for their next delivery rounds.

**I - SPY points: 20**

## MINIBUS

Some schools have their own minibuses, and others are used by Scout groups, sailing clubs and similar organisations. A typical minibus, like this one, is converted from a delivery van with windows and seats added. You can hire one if you need it only occasionally.

**I - SPY points: 10**

## MOBILE BANK

Internet banking is perfect for those who live in remote parts of the UK, but a mobile bank is a great alternative for people without on-line access. This one brings a full range of financial services to villages in far-flung corners of the Highlands. Inside is a proper counter, situated just behind the driver's compartment.

 **I - SPY points: 40**

## MOBILE CRANE

You'll see these amazing vehicles driving, from one construction site to another. They fold up, rather like a Transformer, but when needed the crane can raise and extend telescopically for all kinds of heavy lifting tasks. This six-wheeler, owned by hire company Ainscough, is a typical model.

 **I - SPY points: 25**

## MOBILE LIBRARY

Not everyone lives near a library so many local councils offer a mobile book-borrowing service – they bring the library to you, especially if you live in the countryside. These special truck-based vans are fully kitted out with bookshelves and all the latest titles.

I - SPY points: 25

## MOBILE SNACK BAR

Motorways have service areas, other major roads have cafes and restaurants, but you'll find mobile snack bars in lots of other places. They generally have a serving hatch at the side, with a fold-out canopy and counter, through which your bacon sandwich, fish-and-chips, cup of tea or can of fizzy drink is served.

I - SPY points: 15

## MOPED

Old style mopeds were a low-powered motorcycle with pedals. You won't see many of those today – they're no longer sold. Instead, a modern moped will be like this Yamaha Aerox R, a mini-scooter for commuting that, despite its modest 49cc engine, can still be customised to look cool.

**I - SPY points: 10**

## MOTORCYCLE

This is a Honda Varadero, which only has a 125cc engine but has excellent handling and styling like a bigger sports bike. A streamlined fairing ahead of the handlebars helps shield the rider from the wind. And the rack above the rear wheel can be used to strap on a small item of luggage.

**I - SPY points: 10**

## MOTORCYCLE, TOURING

Some motorbikes are designed for zipping around on but others, like this Triumph Rocket III Classic, are big-engined touring bikes. Large and comfortable, but also powerful, there is plenty of room for two people – the passenger is called a 'pillion' rider.

**I - SPY points: 15**

## MOTORCYCLE COMBINATION

A motorbike with a sidecar is known as a combination. Thanks to appearances in '*Wallace & Gromit*' and '*Harry Potter*' films, you might recognise this classic, bullet-shaped model, made by Britain's Watsonian-Squire. Here, it's paired with a traditional-style 'bike, an Indian-made Royal Enfield.

**I - SPY points: 35**

## MOTORHOME

Many holidaymakers find it easier to drive a motorhome than a car pulling a caravan. This is a Peugeot with an Elddis Explorer conversion, one of the more compact 'coachbuilt' models, but most motorhomes have enough rear headroom for people to stand upright.

I - SPY points: 10

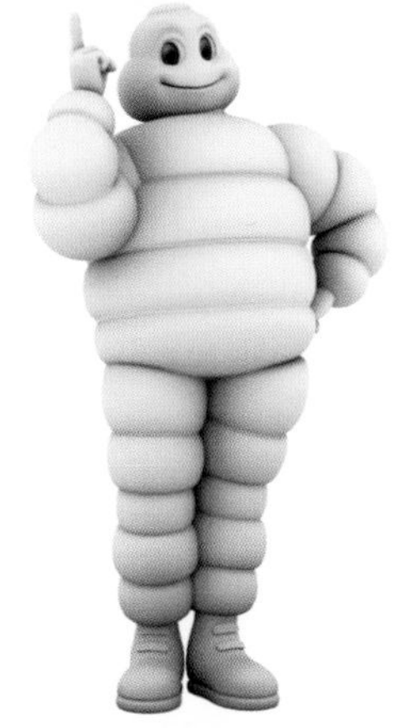

## MULTI-PASSENGER VEHICLE

These cars are packed with features making them ideal for large, busy families. The biggest models have three rows of seats so seven or even nine people can be carried. Several, like this Chrysler Voyager, offer sliding rear passenger doors, and have removable back seats; MPV can also stand for multi-purpose vehicle.

I - SPY points: 10

## PAVEMENT/ROAD CLEANER

You'll see this tiny truck in towns and cities, where it is used by the local council – here's one of Croydon Council's fleet – to suck up rubbish from gutters and pavements. The brushes at the front sweep up and a suction machine underneath pulls it into a collection box at the back. Some machines can also hose down dusty streets with water.

**I - SPY points: 15**

## PICK-UP

At the front, it looks like a normal saloon car, but the bodywork is abruptly ended behind the doors and a large open-topped tray is fitted – the pick-up bed. At the back is a fold-down tailgate. They're widely used for small businesses and in the countryside, where four-wheel drive versions are popular; this is a Toyota Hilux.

**I - SPY points: 10**

## PICK-UP DOUBLE-CAB

This utility vehicle is a useful mixture of car and pick-up truck. There are five proper seats inside the four-door passenger compartment but the shortened pick-up load bay is still spacious enough to carry plenty of stuff. This one is a Mitsubishi L200, with four-wheel drive.

 **I - SPY points: 15**

## POLICE CAR

Britain's forces use similar cars as everyone else, although with heavy-duty suspension and special communications equipment. You can't see those but you can see the reflective 'Police' livery all over the bodywork (usually a white or silver base colour), and the blue flashing warning light unit on the roof.

 **I - SPY points: 10**

## POLICE MOTORBIKE

This motorbike is a BMW 1200 RT, a large, powerful yet nimble sports model that has a proven track record with police riders across Britain. Apart from the eyecatching luminous yellow livery, a police bike is recognisable by its substantial radio antenna on the back, pannier storage units on both sides above the rear wheel, and the blue flashing blue lights on its fairing; plus, of course, the policeman riding it!

 **I - SPY points: 15**

## POSTAL VAN

Like the pillar-box you drop your letters into, the vans used by Britain's national postal service, Royal Mail, are all painted red. Some have a yellow stripe along the side but they all carry the Queen's crown-shaped crest. This Vauxhall Combo is one of Royal Mail's smaller local delivery/ collection vans; it also uses bigger vans, minibuses, light trucks and articulated trucks.

 **I - SPY points: 10**

## PRISONER TRANSPORT VAN

For carrying people between police stations, courts and prisons, a special van like this is used. It is, in effect, a mobile prison cell designed to ensure that criminals can't make their escape. They travel with guards in the back in a secure metal 'cube', built on to the back of a reinforced van cab. Police motorcycles are often used as outriders to clear the way for this type of vehicle.

**I - SPY points: 25**

## QUADBIKE

It looks like a four-wheeled motorbike, and that's exactly what a quadbike is. Although it has the stability of a car, it is steered by handlebars and the rider sits astride a saddle and wears a helmet. They are very useful for farmers and shepherds, the fat tyres and four-wheel drive allowing them to go anywhere.

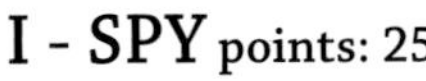

**I - SPY points: 25**

## RADIO CAR

Broadcasters need specially-equipped cars for covering events and on-the-spot news reporting. The enormous antenna on the roof allows journalists to transmit their reports back to the studio. There's usually a webcam camera mounted on the roof, and plenty of room inside to carry equipment, and also to conduct interviews.

**I - SPY points: 40**

## RECOVERY TRUCK, FOR CARS

This is a light commercial vehicle, based on a van or light truck, with a flat bed at the back on to which a broken-down car can be winched. A strong nylon rope is attached to the front of the car, and it's then pulled aboard up a pair of extendable ramps that pull or fold out from the back of the truck. It can then be taken to a garage for repairs.

**I - SPY points: 20**

## RECOVERY TRUCK, FOR TRUCKS AND BUSES

I - SPY points: 25

A broken down truck or bus can cause huge disruption for other drivers. That's when one of these large, strong vehicles is needed. The rear end has a drop-down rig that can be positioned under the front wheels of the stricken bus or truck, and it can then be carefully towed away. It has powerful warning lights on top.

## RECYCLING COLLECTION TRUCK

This van-based vehicle has separate compartments at the back so different categories of rubbish can be carried back to the council depot, to make sorting it out easier. You may see larger vehicles that take away unsorted waste for recycling, but most will carry a recycling slogan along their sides. Score for any 'recycling' vehicle you see.

I - SPY points: 15

## REFRIGERATED/FREEZER VAN

This Citroën has a special 'cool box' on the back designed to carry food that must be kept in freezing or chilled temperatures. You can tell it apart from a normal van because it will have a refrigeration unit either on the main roof or else above the passenger compartment.

I - SPY points: 20

## REFUSE TRUCK

These large, noisy trucks visit your street usually once a week or once a fortnight. A team of refuse collectors throw bags of rubbish into the open-ended rear, and an automatically operated mechanism inside compacts it so as much as possible can be crammed in.

I - SPY points: 15

## REMOVAL VAN

If you've moved house then a huge truck like this probably took care of the job. Removers have special ways to position all your possessions so nothing gets damaged on the journey. Some have a sleeping compartment above the cab.

**I - SPY points: 20**

## RICKSHAW/BIKE TAXI

Three- and four-wheeled rickshaws are a tourist attraction as taxis around central London. The passengers sit at the back under a canopy while the 'driver' is at the front, steering with handlebars and providing all the power – through pedals! They are the ultimate in zero-emission transport.

**I - SPY points: 35**

## ROAD-SWEEPER

The rounded tank at the back is filled with water; the driver sprays this on to the road and uses the brushes at the sides to collect the rubbish, at the same time damping down dust and cleaning the road. As they move slowly, there is normally a flashing orange light on top.

I - SPY points: 15

## SALOON CAR, FOUR-DOOR

This is the traditional shape of car. It's known as a 'three-box' car: there's one large box in the middle for the passengers, a smaller box sticking out of the front containing the engine, and another smaller box jutting out at the back which is the luggage compartment.

I - SPY points: 5

I - SPY points: 5

## SALOON CAR, TWO-DOOR

A two-door saloon with the same three-box profile will still have at least four seats, the rear ones accessed by tipping the front seats forward. This style of car, typified by the BMW M3 shown here, tends to be aimed less at families and more at drivers who like sporty performance. That's why many two-door saloons are marketed as coupés.

## SCAFFOLDING TRUCK

To carry the long steel poles of scaffolding, special flat trucks or trailers are required. Around the edges of the flatbed load area are uprights that stop the poles rolling off when they're being transported. These trucks also carry the metal joints that allow vertical and horizontal poles to be joined securely together, when renovating buildings.

I - SPY points: 15

## SCHOOL BUS

Local councils organise special bus services to take children to school – maybe you use one. This bus operates on the Scottish island of Islay in the Hebrides. School buses in the USA are all painted yellow; in the UK, the way to spot one is to look for the yellow 'School' sign in the window or the words 'School Service' on the destination board.

**I - SPY points: 10**

## SCOOTER

These compact motorcycles are very popular for commuting, as they can beat traffic jams and use minimal fuel. This one is Yamaha's BW125. It's typical of the modern scooter in that it has sleek styling but is simple to use.

**I - SPY points: 10**

## SECURITY VAN

Seems like a basic delivery van but look closely and you'll see it's been toughened up with double rear wheels, armour-plated doors and thick bullet-proof glass. It also has side-mounted video cameras and hefty protective strips and wheelarches. It's all to make the van more secure as it collects and delivers money and other valuables.

 **I - SPY points: 20**

## SKIP TRUCK

Skips are huge, metal buckets that can be delivered and collected by trucks like this six-wheeled DAF CF, which has a special hydraulic lifting mechanism at the back to lift the skip on and off. The weight it can lift is awesome!

 **I - SPY points: 15**

## SNOWPLOUGH

Some councils and highways agencies keep snowploughs on standby in winter and you probably will see one after a thick and sudden snowfall. The big blade at the front is specially curved to lift snow off the road and push it aside. These trucks often have a gritter unit on the back.

**I - SPY points: 40**

## SPORTS CAR

A sports car has two seats and a folding fabric (although sometimes metal) roof. This makes it great fun for journeys on fine days. Sports cars, like this Mazda MX-5, are built close to the ground, and the low centre of gravity helps it corner at high speed.

**I - SPY points: 15**

## SPORT-UTILITY VEHICLE

Most people call them simply SUVs. These tall cars almost all have four-wheel drive, big wheels and high ground clearance, so they perform excellently off-road. Today, they use conventional road car technology for suspension and chassis, so the latest SUVs drive well on the road too.

**I - SPY points: 15**

## SUPERCAR

This Lamborghini Gallardo Spyder is a typical supercar: there are two seats in a wedge-shaped body, and the high-performance engine behind the cockpit but in front of the rear wheels – just like in a pure racing car. Supercars like this and also Ferraris, Porsches, Aston Martins and McLarens are capable of speeds of over 200mph.

**I - SPY points: 40**

## SUPERMARKET DELIVERY VAN

Most supermarkets have a home-delivery service for internet shoppers, so they need special vans to bring groceries to our doors. They all carry advertisements on their sides but another identifying feature is the refrigeration unit above the cab, to keep the contents chilled.

**I - SPY points: 10**

## SUPERMINI

The term 'supermini' arose in the early 1970s, when car designers tried to improve the original, fun-to-drive Mini but with more space and practicality, by including a hatchback rear door and folding back seats. They proved amazingly popular, and still are now.

**I - SPY points: 10**

## TANDEM

This is the name for a bicycle built for two people. They are great for cycling holidays, and some enthusiasts even race them. The person on the front has to trust the person behind is pulling their weight; likewise, the person on the back relies on their friend upfront to steer and brake!

**I - SPY points: 30**

## TAXI

Britain is one of the few countries that builds a special taxi, rather than a converted car. A 25ft turning circle means it can tackle narrow streets in London, where most of them operate. Notice the roof sign; when it's not lit, the taxi is in use, when it's illuminated it's available for hire. If you need a taxi, you have to wave to the driver.

**I - SPY points: 5**

## THREE-WHEELED CAR, FRONT SINGLE WHEEL

This Reliant Robin was the UK's most popular three-wheeler. It's very light, with plastic bodywork, which means, legally, it's classed as a tricycle and can be driven on a motorbike licence. Last on sale in 2002, owners still like it because it's economical and rustproof.

**I - SPY points: 25**

## THREE-WHEELED CAR, BACK SINGLE WHEEL

Much less common than a Reliant-type three-wheeler is a car with its single wheel behind the driving seat. This British-made Triking might look odd but it's similar to three-wheeled sports cars of the 1920s and '30s. It has a powerful motorbike engine sticking out of the front and, with a little practice, is great fun to drive.

**I - SPY points: 50**

## THREE-WHEELED DELIVERY VAN

The tiny cab has room for just one person, who steers with handlebars as on a scooter. The engine of this Piaggio is small and its performance is slow, but the van's small size makes it brilliant for light deliveries in cities. Very popular in Italy, they are now catching on in the UK too.

 **I - SPY points: 50**

## TIPPER

This eight-wheeled ERF is one of the biggest tipper trucks you'll see on the road. Its big open container at the back can tip out its massive load of loose material such as sand, gravel or stones using a heavyweight hydraulic ram behind the cab. At the back, a hinged tailgate swings open to regulate the flow.

 **I - SPY points: 20**

## TRACTOR

Tractors come in different sizes and styles, but most feature huge rear wheels with knobbly tyres and a glass-sided cab from where the driver has an all-round view. This is essential because it may be called upon to tow trailers, plough fields or dig trenches.

**I - SPY points: 10**

## TRACTOR CAB

Not to be confused with an agricultural tractor, these units are the power houses that pull containers and flat beds around the country. They can look quite strange when they are travelling without pulling a load – but they are probably just in between jobs!

**I - SPY points: 20**

## TRAILER, FOR DOMESTIC USE

This Indespension Daxara trailer is a British-made model extremely popular with active people. It can be attached to the back of any car that has a tow hook, and plugs into the car's electric system to power its lights. Very handy carrying holiday luggage or camping gear.

I - SPY points: 10

## TRAM

A tram is half bus, half train. Like a bus, it travels along city streets, but like a train its concealed wheels run in tracks and it draws its power from overhead electricity cables. Trams are usually articulated in two or three sections.

I - SPY points: 15

## UNIMOG

The Unimog has been manufactured for many years in Germany by Mercedes-Benz. It is a tall four-wheel drive truck that combines pick-up and tractor abilities. The base unit can be fitted with many kinds of bodies, and power take-off (PTO) points mean it can perform unusual tasks, like roadside hedge-cutting as shown here.

**I - SPY points: 50**

## VAN

You will see vans like this Ford Transit, the most popular of its type in the UK, absolutely everywhere. They are simple workhorses with an integrated cab and load area, and come with two, side-opening back doors or, sometimes, a lifting tailgate. Other models are LDVs, Peugeots, Renaults, Vauxhalls and Volkswagens.

**I - SPY points: 5**

# VETERAN CAR

Owners treasure these ancient cars from the veteran period, which ran from 1885 to around 1905. Every year, the London-Brighton Veteran Car Run on the first Sunday in November is the place to see lots of them. It might look like a sewing machine on wheels, but this was an extremely modern car in 1900!

**I - SPY points: 50**

# VINTAGE CAR

Vintage cars were made from 1918 until 1930, at a time when few British people could afford a car. They are very valuable among collectors. You're most likely to see one at a car show in the summer.

**I - SPY points: 40**

## WALK-THROUGH DELIVERY VAN

This is a large van used by laundry companies and courier services. Its height is necessary so the delivery driver, who will make many calls over a working day, can easily walk into the rear compartment from the driving seat, to pick up a package carried in a racking system.

 I - SPY points: 20

## WIDE LOAD ARTICULATED TRUCK

This vehicle is a monster low-loader for carrying things that are extra-wide, such as this enormous truck designed for use in a mine. It is very low to the ground and has a large number of wheels to spread the weight. If you see something like this driving slowly along a motorway it sometimes has a police escort in order to prevent other traffic getting too close.

 I - SPY points: 30

# Index




First published by Michelin Maps and Guides 2011



Created and produced by Blue Sky Publishing Limited.



Printed in China.

The publisher gratefully acknowledges the contribution of the I-Spy team: Camilla Lovell, Ruth Neilson and Geoff Watts in the production of this title.

The publisher gratefully acknowledges the contribution of Giles Chapman, who compiled the contents and wrote the text.

The majority of the photographs in this book are sourced from the manufacturers of the vehicles pictured. The publisher also gratefully acknowledges, in particular, the helpful assistance of Gemma Woodall (Ainscough Crane Hire), Martyn Weston (BBC Radio Norfolk), John Bownas (London Borough Of Croydon), Harriet McCaw (for Dairy Crest), Neil Singleton (Indespension trailers), Keith Child (Isuzu Truck UK), Jane Cornwall (JCB), Simon Wood (Mercedes-Benz UK), David Rowlands (for Optare), Steve Blakeley (Pennine Leisure convertible caravans), Mike Gale (Renault UK), Simon Alton (Shropshire Council) Nicki Layzell (Triking), Rossana Tich (for Reva G-Wiz), Ben Matthews (Watsonian-Squire) and Ed Whitby (Whitby-Morrison ice-cream vans) for assistance in providing relevant images. Thanks to Spencer Chapman (aged 8) for his help with picture choice. Additional photographs were supplied by the Giles Chapman Library and Unitaw Limited.



Reprinted 2014 12 11 10 9 8 7 6 5

# HOW TO GET YOUR I-SPY CERTIFICATE AND BADGE

*Every time you score 1000 points or more in an I-Spy book, you can apply for a certificate*

## HERE'S WHAT TO DO, STEP BY STEP:

### *Certificate*

- Ask an adult to check your score
- Ask his or her permission to apply for a certificate
- Apply online to www.ispymichelin.com
- Enter your name and address and the completed title
- We will send you back via e mail your certificate for the title

### *Badge*

- Each I-Spy title has a cut out (page corner) token at the back of the book
- Collect five tokens from different I-Spy titles
- Put Second Class Stamps on two strong envelopes
- Write your own address on one envelope and put a £1 coin inside it (for protection). Fold, but do not seal the envelope, and place it inside the second envelope
- Write the following address on the second envelope, seal it carefully and post to:

I-Spy Books
Michelin Maps and Guides
Hannay House
39 Clarendon Road
Watford
WD17 1JA